Logical Thinking Puzzles

Paul Sloane & Des MacHale

•••

Illustrated by Myron Miller

 Sterling Publishing Co., Inc.   New York

With acknowledgments to Ajaz Ahmed for "Deduction,"
Andy Balchin for "How to Hug," and Erwin Brecher for
"The Stranger in the Car."

Edited by Claire Bazinet

Library of Congress Cataloging-in-Publication Data

Sloane, Paul, 1950–
    Logical thinking puzzles / by Paul Sloane and Des MacHale :
illustrated by Myron Miller.
       p.   cm.
    Includes index.
    ISBN 0-8069-8670-0
    1. Puzzles.   2. Logic.   I. MacHale, Des.   II. Title.
GV1493.S5945   1992
793.73—dc20   92-19095
                                        CIP

10 9 8 7 6 5 4 3 2 1

Published by Sterling Publishing Company, Inc.
387 Park Avenue South, New York, N.Y. 10016
© 1992 by Paul Sloane and Des MacHale
Distributed in Canada by Sterling Publishing
% Canadian Manda Group, P.O. Box 920, Station U
Toronto, Ontario, Canada M8Z 5P9
Distributed in Great Britain and Europe by Cassell PLC
Villiers House, 41/47 Strand, London WC2N 5JE, England
Distributed in Australia by Capricorn Link Ltd.
P.O. Box 665, Lane Cove, NSW 2066
Manufactured in the United States of America
All rights reserved

Sterling ISBN 0-8069-8670-0

*This book is dedicated
to our long-suffering wives,
Ann Sloane and Anne MacHale,
in appreciation
of their patience and support.*

CONTENTS

INTRODUCTION

It is said that when the North American Indians first saw a man riding a horse they assumed that it was some new creature with four legs and two arms. Very often when we face a new situation or problem we fall back on prior experiences and form quick but incorrect judgments. We assume too much, ask too few questions, and jump to the wrong conclusions.

This book should provide an amusing antidote to any bad habits of lazy or inflexible thinking. The puzzles will probably provide the most entertainment and brain-flexing value if attempted in a small group. One person knows the solution and the others, whether family, friends, or colleagues, ask questions in order to determine the answer. In the strictest form of this game the "Chairperson" can give one of three answers, only, to any question: yes, no, or irrelevant. The most successful questioners are those who are imaginative and logical, who test all assumptions and then try to narrow down the area of search with broad questions before homing in on specific details. In the right company, the game can be frustrating, stimulating, hilarious, and rewarding.

The puzzles generally do not have obscure solutions or need specialist knowledge. They are not designed to deliberately mislead the reader. The exceptions are the "WALLY Tests," which consist of special questions employing every low trick to catch you out.

These puzzles are meant to test your powers of questioning, deduction, and persistence. If at first the direct approach leads nowhere, try coming at the problem from the side; in other words, lateral thinking. Be flexible. Don't look straight at the answers or you will miss most of the fun. When you do get frustrated try the clues section for some help. Remember that in real life there are no answers at the back of the book. Enjoy the puzzles!

THE PUZZLES

1   Easy Puzzles

1.1   The Apple Problem

There were six apples in a basket and six girls in the room.
Each girl took one apple, yet one apple remained in the
basket. How come?

1.2   The Two Presidents

The 22nd and 24th presidents of the United States had the same mother and the same father, but were not brothers. How could this be so?

1.3   Game, Set, and Match

Two men were playing tennis. They played five sets and each man won three sets. How did they do this?

1.4   Wondrous Walk

A man walked all the way from Dublin to Cork along main roads without passing a single pub. How did he manage that? (Pubs or "public houses," that is, bars, are very common in Ireland.)

1.5   Father and Son

William's father was older than his grandfather. How did that happen?

1.6   The Amazing Fall

A man who was not wearing a parachute jumped out of a plane. He landed on hard ground yet he was unhurt. Why?

1.7   Shopping Is Good for You

A man got up at 9 a.m. He became so engrossed in his newspaper he did not have time to go out and shop as he had planned. At 11 a.m. he went for a flying lesson. He carefully followed all the instructions given to him by his instructor until he came in to land. He then ignored his instructor and crashed the plane killing them both. The accident would not have happened if he had gone shopping, which just goes to show how important shopping can be. Why should this be so?

1.8   Your Turn to Drive

Two brothers were talking. One said, "I am fed up with living in Birmingham because I have to drive all the time. Why don't we move to London?" His brother replied, "But that would mean that I would have to drive all the time." Why was this true?

1.9   See Saw

A deaf man needed to buy a saw to cut some wood. He went into a hardware store. How did he indicate to the storekeeper that he wanted to buy a saw?

1.10 The Two Lookouts

Two sentries were on duty outside a barracks. One faced up the road to watch for anyone approaching from the north. The other looked down the road to see if anyone approached from the south. Suddenly one of them said to the other, "Why are you smiling?" How did he know that his companion was smiling?

1.11 The Deadly Drive

A man drove to and from work every day along a dangerous and twisty mountain road. However, he knew the road very well so could drive quickly yet safely. One day, while he was at work, his car was broken into and several items were stolen. As the car was not damaged the man got in and started driving. He never reached home. His car swerved off the road and he was killed. Why?

1.12 Another Man in an Elevator

Bill was on holiday. He stayed on the fifth floor of a hotel. Every morning at 8 a.m. he took the elevator down to the lobby on the first floor, had breakfast, and then took the elevator back up to the fifth floor. Every evening at 8 p.m. he took the elevator down to the lobby and then he walked up the five flights of stairs and went back to his room. He did not like walking up all those stairs, so why did he do it?

1.13 Growing Younger

Ben was 20 years old in 1980 but only 15 years old in 1985. How come?

1.14 The Habitual Walker

A deaf man was very regular in his habits. He arose every morning at 7:35 a.m. and set off for his half-hour morning walk at 7:45. In the course of this walk he went over a level railroad crossing but he knew that he was quite safe because the first train did not come by until 9 a.m. One morning, although he followed his routine exactly, he was run over by a train at the crossing. What went wrong?

1.15 Greenland

Greenland is a huge country covered with snow and ice. Why did the man who discovered it call it Greenland?

1.16 Radio On

A young girl was listening to the radio. Suddenly it went off for a minute and then came back on again. There was nothing wrong with the radio or with the program transmission from the radio station. She did not touch the radio controls. Why did it go off and on?

1.17   The Boxing Match

At the end of a long hard boxing match one boxer was knocked out by the other. The judges agreed it was a completely proper victory. Yet during the course of the match no man threw a punch. What happened?

1.18   The Nephew

A man and his sister were out shopping one day when the man said, ''That boy over there is my nephew.'' ''That is right,'' replied his sister, ''but he is not my nephew.'' How come?

1.19   Barrel Trouble

A man filled an empty barrel. It was then lighter than when he started. What did he fill it with?

1.20   Rival Fans

One day, in a crowded room, a supporter of the Brazilian soccer team saw a supporter of his team's great rivals, Argentina. The Brazilian fan walked over to the Argentinian fan and struck him a fierce blow. The Argentinian fan who had been knocked flat got up from the floor, turned around, and then thanked the man who had hit him. Why?

1.21   Coming Up for Air

As part of a school experiment a girl was sent to the middle of a nearby city with instructions to collect a sample so that pollution levels could be measured. She was given a glass container with a removable but tight-fitting lid. Of course she noticed that the jar contained comparatively clean air from the school environment. How did she ensure that she excluded this air and retrieved an absolutely accurate sample of the city air?

1.22   Nuts Away!

A man was changing a wheel on his car when the four nuts used to hold the wheel in place fell into a sewer drain and were lost. He was afraid he was stuck there, but a passing boy made a very useful suggestion which enabled the man to drive off. What was the boy's idea?

1.23   The Golf Pro

Although there are very few golf tour professionals who are left-handed, most clubs prefer to have left-handed golf pros as instructors. Why?

1.24 Deduction

A man suspected his wife of having an affair. One day he told her that he had been suddenly called away on business and would be out of town for a few days. He then left the house but returned an hour later. His wife was not there but he quickly discovered the name and address of her lover. How?

The WALLY Test

Now that you have warmed up with the Easy Puzzles you are ready to try your wits on the first official World Association for Laughter, Learning, and Youth (WALLY) Test. Get a pencil and paper. You must answer each question immediately after reading it. You have 4 minutes to complete the test and you are not allowed to change any answer once it is written. Do not look at the solutions until you have answered all the questions.

(a) Write your name in the square provided.

(b) Take two apples from five apples. How many do you have?

(c) Do they have Fourth of July in England?

(d) If you had only one match and entered a dark room containing an oil lamp, a newspaper, and some kindling wood, what would you light first?

(e) A farmer had 17 sheep. All but 9 died. How many did he have left?

(f) How many animals of each species did Moses take into the Ark?

(g) A plane full of English tourists flies from Holland to Spain. It crashes in France. Where should the survivors be buried?

(h) If a redhouse is made of red wood and a whitehouse is made of white wood, what is a greenhouse made of?

(i) If Mr. Jones' peacock laid an egg in Mr. Brown's garden, who is the rightful owner of the egg?

(j) Mrs. Taylor's bungalow is decorated entirely in pink. Her lamps, walls, carpets, and ceilings are all pink. What color are her stairs?

(k) If you drive a bus with 42 people on board from Boston to Washington, D.C., and drop off 3 people at each of six stops and pick up 4 people at half the stops, when you arrive at Washington 10 hours later what is the driver's name?

(l) Write this down as one number: 15 thousand, 15 hundred, and 15.

(m) What do Kermit the Frog and Attila the Hun have in common?

(n) What do you sit on, sleep on, and brush your teeth with?

(o) How many times can you take 3 from 25?

See WALLY Test solution on page 18.

2 Moderate Puzzles

2.1 The Penny Black

The famous Penny Black, the world's first postage stamp, was introduced in England in 1840. The idea of postage stamps was a great success and was taken up worldwide. Yet the Penny Black was in use for only one year before it was replaced by the Penny Red. Why?

2.2 Flat Tire I

A man woke up one morning to find that one of the wheels of his car had a completely flat tire. Despite this he set off in his car and drove 100 miles to visit a customer. He then drove 100 miles home. He did not repair or inflate the flat tire. How did he manage to make the journey?

2.3 Flat Tire II

Four college students arrived late for a lecture, explaining to their instructor that their car had suffered a flat tire on the way there. How did the clever lecturer immediately show those assembled that the late arrivals were not telling the truth?

2.4 Bottled Fruit

We all know that there's a way to get a ship into a bottle. How would you get a full-sized pear into a bottle without damaging the pear or breaking or cutting the bottle?

2.5 The Cowboy's Fate

Cowboys who lived in the Wild West led a dangerous existence. They were at risk from cattle stampedes, Indian attacks, rattlesnakes, disease, and gunfights. However, none of these was the usual cause of death, which was something routine but deadly. What was the most common cause of death among cowboys?

2.6 The Village Idiot

Visitors to a scenic mountain village were often amused by the village idiot. When offered a choice between a shiny 50-cent piece and a crumpled $5 bill, he would always happily choose the half-dollar. The bill was worth ten times as much, so why did he never choose it?

2.7 The Island Fire

A man is on an island which is one mile long and about 100 yards wide. The grass and shrubs are very dry from a long drought. Suddenly, a fire starts at one end of the island. It is racing towards him along the width of the island fanned by a strong wind blowing in his direction. He cannot take refuge in the sea because it is infested with sharks. There is no beach, just sheer cliffs. What can he do to avoid being consumed in the flames?

2.8 The Sleepy Kings

On one occasion King George II of England went to sleep on the night of September 2 and did not wake up until the morning of September 14. His doctors and advisors were not particularly worried by this. Maybe this was because they knew that a similar sort of thing had once happened to King Henry III of France. He had fallen asleep on December 9 and not woken until December 20. We know that monarchs in those days had a pretty easy life, but what was going on here?

2.9 The Portrait

A man stands looking at a portrait and says, "Sons and brothers have I none, but this person's father is my father's son." Who is in the portrait?

The WALLY Test Answers

Total up your number of correct answers. Then see where you fit on this table:

Score	Official Rating
10–15	Smart Alec
5–9	Wally
0–4	Mega Wally

(o) Once.
(n) A chair, a bed, and a toothbrush.
(m) The same middle name—"the."
(l) 16,515.
(k) Your name.
(j) There are no stairs in a bungalow.
(i) Peacocks do not lay eggs.
(h) Glass.
(g) Survivors are not buried.
(f) None (it was Noah's Ark).
(e) Nine.
(p) The match.
(c) Yes.
(b) Two apples.
(a) What square?

18

2.10 Winning Isn't Everything

Three friends, Alf, Bert, and Chris, played golf every Saturday for a year. The games were friendly but competitive. They all had the same handicap so whoever took the least strokes won the game and whoever took the most strokes came last. At the end of the year they compared scores to see who was the best and a furious row broke out. Alf pointed out that he had finished ahead of Bert more often than he had finished behind him. Bert countered that he had finished ahead of Chris more often than he had finished behind him and that Chris had finished ahead of Alf more often than he had finished behind him. How could this be so?

2.11 The Reluctant Diner

A businessman came home as usual at 5 P.M. He normally ate dinner as soon as he arrived home. This evening he was very hungry as he had had no lunch. However, despite the fact that all his favorite foods were available and ready to be eaten, he waited until exactly 8 P.M. before dining alone. Why did he wait?

2.12 Death in a Car

A man went out for a drive. A day later he was found dead in the car. The car had not crashed. How had he died?

2.13 Last Cord

A man lies dead in a field. Next to him is a long piece of cord. How did he die?

2.14 Saturday Flights

A man flew into Los Angeles on Saturday. He stayed for three nights at the Beverly Hills Hotel, then spent one night in the Santa Monica Hilton. He then flew out again on Saturday. Between the two flights he never left the Los Angeles area and he did not stay anywhere except those two hotels. How could he arrive and leave on Saturday, yet stay only four nights?

2.15 The Trains That Did Not Crash

A single train track runs through a tunnel which goes from east to west. One afternoon two trains run along the track at the same speed and enter the tunnel, one going east and the other going west. Neither stops or changes speed, yet they do not crash. Why not?

2.16 Copyright

How do the publishers of dictionaries or atlases protect themselves from pirates who would copy their work?

20

2.17 The Ransom

A rich man's son was kidnapped. The ransom note told him to bring a valuable diamond to a phone booth in the middle of a public park. Plainclothes police officers surrounded the park, intending to follow the criminal or his messenger. The rich man arrived at the phone booth and followed instructions but the police were powerless to prevent the diamond from leaving the park and reaching the crafty villain. What did he do?

2.18 Moving Parts

Two common objects carry out the same function. One of the objects has many thousands of moving parts while the other object has no moving parts. What are the objects?

2.19 An Early Burial

John Brown died on Thursday, December 6, and was buried the same week—on Wednesday, December 5, to be precise. How did that happen?

2.20 Trouble and Strife

Mrs. White was happily knitting while her husband watched television. Suddenly the phone rang. Mr. White answered it. He was angry because it was a wrong number, but she was even more angry. Why?

2.21 Bath Water

Some time ago, before central heating and water boilers, people would heat water on stoves. At that time a scullery maid was heating a large pan of water in order to add it to a bathtub which contained some water at room temperature. When the butler saw it he told her off. "Don't you realize," he said, "that the longer you heat that water on the stove the colder the bath will be when you pour the hot water in?" He was right. Why?

2.22 The Hold-Up

A man parked his car outside a bank and rushed in. He held up twenty-five people and ran out with $200. A policeman who saw the whole incident stopped the man. He told him off and then let him go. Why?

2.23 The Worst Sailor

Jim was one of the worst sailors on board ship. He was surly, lazy, untrustworthy, uncooperative, and always causing trouble. Yet the ship's captain often said of him, "I wish we had ten men like Jim." Why?

2.24 The Valuable Book

A man had a book which was worth $40,000. Why did he deliberately destroy it?

3 Difficult Puzzles

3.1 Cuddly Bears

At a children's hospital the patients loved to play with the cuddly teddy bears they had there. Unfortunately, the children liked them so much that the bears were disappearing at an alarming rate as the young patients took them home. How did the hospital solve this problem?

3.2 The High-Society Dinner

At a fancy, upper-class dinner party a precious gold coin was being passed around the table for inspection when suddenly the lights went out. When the lights came on again the coin was missing. A search of each guest was ordered. One man refused to be searched. The police were called but before they arrived the missing coin was found under a saucer. Why did the guest refuse to be searched?

3.3 Eight Years Old

A girl was eight years old on her first birthday. How could that be?

3.4 Cover That Hole

A manhole is a hole which allows someone to gain access to the sewers or other pipes which are below ground. Our local town council recently decided that all the town's manhole covers should be changed from square to round ones. We are used to the town council making silly decisions, but this time they were absolutely right. Why?

3.5 The Protagoras Paradox

Protagoras was a lawyer in ancient Greece. As an act of kindness he took on a poor but promising young man as a pupil. He agreed to teach him law but make no charge until the student had won his first case, when the student would repay his tuition fees. The young man gladly agreed to this plan. The student completed his training, then decided that he did not wish to practise law. Instead, he retired to the countryside to keep goats. Protagoras was disgusted at this waste of talent and training and dismayed that he would not be reimbursed for the tuition. He decided to sue his pupil in order to recover his fees. If the two men met in court to argue the case, who do you think would have won?

24

3.6 Hand in Glove
· ·

A French glove manufacturer received an order for 5,000 pairs of expensive sealskin gloves from a New York department store. He then learned that there was a very expensive tax on the import of sealskin gloves into the United States. How did he (legitimately) get the gloves into the country without paying the import tax?

3.7 The School Superintendent
· ·

A visiting school superintendent noticed that whenever he asked one class a question all the children would put up their hands. Moreover, although the teacher always chose a different child to answer, the answer was always correct. Why?

3.8   No Trumps

Can you resolve this argument which arose at a recent bridge match? Spades were trumps. Which is more likely: that a pair of players will have no spades dealt to them or all the spades dealt to them?

3.9   How to Beat Nick Faldo

A man challenged the Masters Golf champion to a round of golf on the condition that he be allowed to chose the time and place of their contest. The champion accepted the challenge but was easily defeated by the challenger. Why?

3.10   How to Beat Carl Lewis

A man challenged the Olympic 100-metres sprint champion to a race over a short distance on the condition that he be allowed to choose the course. How does the man manage to beat the champion? (N.B.: The solution to the preceding problem won't help you here.)

3.11   The Missing Furniture

A man was doing his job but was killed because he lacked a certain piece of furniture. Why?

3.12   The Dead Man

A man lies dead in a room, with a cord tied tightly around his neck. The door has been locked from the inside. Outside of the body, there is nothing else in the room. Remembering that one cannot choke oneself (one would pass out before dying), how did he die?

3.13   The Busy Hospital

St. James Hospital handled all the accident cases for the

city. They were kept especially busy by the large number of drivers and passengers injured on the city's roads. To improve road safety, a law was passed making the wearing of seat belts mandatory. Drivers and passengers now started to wear seat belts in their cars. The frequency of road accidents remained exactly the same. However, the hospital was now even busier handling road-accident victims than before. Why?

3.14 The Fallen Sign

A man was walking in country unfamiliar to him. He came to a crossroads where he found that the signpost showing the directions of the roads had fallen over. How did he find out which way to go?

3.15   False Fingerprints

A man stabbed his wife to death. He was alone with his victim before and after the crime. To throw the police off the scent he suddenly decided to leave false fingerprints on the murder weapon. How did he do it?

3.16   Found, Lost, Found

A man threw something away. He then paid someone else twenty dollars to try to find it but the search was unsuccessful. Later the man found it easily himself. How?

3.17   The Crippled Child

A child was born with its legs so wasted that it would never be able to walk. When they learned this, the child's parents were especially happy that the child was crippled rather than normal and healthy. Why?

3.18   Insurance

A man's lifelong ambition was to achieve a certain goal, yet he insured himself against achieving it. What was the goal?

3.19   Eggs

Ornithologists now agree that there is a very good reason why birds' eggs are generally narrower at one end than the other. What is the reason?

3.20   The Guard Dog

A landowner boasted that nobody could enter his orchard because of the fierce dog he had guarding it. How did a crafty boy safely gain entrance without damaging the dog in any way?

3.21   The Last Message

A man was found shot dead in his study. He was slumped over his desk and a gun was in his hand. There was a cassette recorder on his desk. When the police entered the room and pressed the play button on the tape recorder they heard, "I can't go on. I have nothing to live for." Then there was the sound of a gunshot. How did the detective immediately know that the man had been murdered?

3.22   The Japanese Speaker

A Los Angeles businessman took great pains to learn Japanese from a native speaker of the language. He became fluent; his vocabulary and grammar were excellent and his accent was good. When he later went to Japan and started speaking Japanese with a group of businessmen there, they could hardly contain their surprise and amusement at the way he spoke. Why?

The Advanced WALLY Test

Before you tackle the next section, Fiendish Puzzles, let's see what you have learned. Get a pencil and paper. You have 4 minutes to complete this advanced WALLY test and you are not allowed to change any answer once it is written. Do not look at the solutions until you have answered all the questions.

(a) John is a popular boys' name in the United States, and many Spanish boys are called José. What is a boy commonly called in France?

(b) To enter the water, why do scuba divers sit on the edge of the boat and fall out backwards?

(c) Is it legal to marry your widow's sister?

(d) If you started in Houston, Texas, to dig a hole through the center of the earth where would you come out?

29

(e) If folk is spelled F O L K and joke is spelled J O K E, how do you spell the word for the white of an egg?

(f) You have two notes in your wallet for a total of $101. One of them is not a $1 bill. What are they?

(g) What could you be sure to find right in the middle of Toronto?

(h) A daddy bull drinks 10 gallons of water per hour and a baby bull drinks 4 gallons. How much would a mommy bull drink?

(i) Who was the last man to box Joe Louis?

(j) Is it likely or unlikely that the next U.S. men's tennis champion will have more than the average number of arms?

(k) A man was walking across a bridge in Paris when he saw his wife on the other side of the bridge with her lover. The man drew a gun and shot his wife. The recoil from the gun caused him to fall off the bridge and drown. He was tried for murder. What was the jury's verdict?

(l) How many grooves are there on the average long-playing record?

(m) Some months have 30 days and some have 31 days. How many have 28 days?

(n) Farmer Giles has three black pigs, two brown pigs, and one pink pig. How many of Farmer Giles' pigs could say that they are the same color as another of Farmer Giles' pigs?

(o) A rope ladder over the side of a ship has rungs which are 1 foot (.3 metres) apart. Exactly 11 rungs are showing above the water level. The tide rose 8 feet (2.4 metres); how many rungs would now be showing?

See Advanced WALLY Test solution on page 35.

4 Fiendish Puzzles

4.1 The Cellar Door

A little girl was warned by her parents never to open the cellar door or she would see things that she was not meant to see. One day while her parents were out she did open the cellar door. What did she see?

4.2 The Deadly Shot

A man lay dead in a field. Next to him was a gun. One shot had been fired and because of that shot the man had died. Yet he had not been shot. In fact, there was no wound or mark on his body. How had he died?

4.3 Flat Out

A driver whose car had no brakes was approaching a level crossing at 60 miles per hour while a train was approaching the same crossing also at 60 miles per hour. The crossing was unmanned and had no barriers. The train was 100 yards long and it was 50 yards from the crossing. The car was 100 yards from the crossing. Neither train nor car stopped or changed direction or speed. The driver did not get out of his car. How did he survive the crossing?

4.4 An Odd Story

Three men went into a cafe and each had a single cup of coffee. Each put an odd number of lumps of sugar into his cup of coffee. In total they put 12 lumps of sugar in their cups. How many lumps did each consume?

4.5 Free Maps

At some stage between the two world wars, the British government decided that it would be desirable to produce accurate maps of the whole country by using the new technique of aerial photography. They were very concerned that the cost of the project would be high as it involved many flights, much film, and long hours of painstaking matching of photographs. In the end the whole process ended up costing the government nothing. Why not?

4.6   What a Shock I

A man woke up. He lit a match. He saw something and died of shock. What was going on?

4.7   What a Shock II

A man was searching a trunk in the attic when he found something that caused him to drop dead of fright. What did he find?

4.8   The Deadly Party

A man went to a party and drank some of the punch. He then left early. Everyone else at the party who drank the punch subsequently died of poisoning. Why did the man not die?

4.9   Speechless

Two men who were good friends had not seen each other for several years. One afternoon they met but they did not speak to each other. Neither was deaf or dumb and there was no prohibition on speaking in the place where they met. Why did they not speak to each other?

4.10   How to Hug

A boy was about to go on his first date. Since he had never embraced a girl before he was anxious to learn a little about how to do it. He went to his local public library and

32

saw a book entitled *How to Hug*. He took it home to read and was greatly disappointed; it gave him no useful advice at all. Why not?

4.11 The Healthy Dairymaids

In the eighteenth century a disease called smallpox was responsible for the deaths of millions of people worldwide. The man whom we can thank for defeating the scourge of smallpox is Edward Jenner, an English country doctor who lived from 1749 to 1823. He noticed that dairymaids never caught smallpox. From this observation he went on to develop a treatment to prevent smallpox and thereby became one of the world's most famous doctors. Why did dairymaids never catch smallpox?

4.12 Toothache

A man was suffering from a toothache so he went to a dentist and had two bad teeth removed. The dentist had done a good job and the man was pleased that he was no longer in pain. Some time later, in a court case, judgment was rendered against the man and he was forced to pay damages to a third party because he had had those teeth removed. Why should that have been so? (Incidentally, the dentist was not at fault and was not involved in the court case.)

4.13 The Lake Problem

There is a large irregularly shaped lake on your estate. It is of variable and unknown depth. There are no rivers or streams entering or leaving the lake. How would you find the volume of water in the lake?

4.14 The Realization

A man was walking downstairs in a building when he suddenly realized that his wife had just died. How?

4.15 The Deadly Dish

Two men went into a restaurant. They both ordered the same dish from the menu. After they tasted it one of the men immediately got up from the table, went outside of the restaurant, and shot himself. Why?

4.16 Men in Uniform

Two men are in the back of a van which is parked on a country road. Both men are in uniform. One is dead. The other is angry and frustrated. What happened?

34

The Advanced WALLY Test Answers

Total up your number of correct answers. Then see how you rate below:

Score	Official Rating
12–15	Smart Alec
7–11	Wally
0–6	Mega Wally

The correct answers are as follows:

(a) *Un garçon.*

(b) Because if they fell forward they would land in the boat!

(c) No. The only way you can have a widow is to be dead.

(d) You would come out near where you started. It is not possible to dig through the earth's molten core.

(e) A L B U M E N

(f) They are a $1 note and a $100 note. (One of them is not a $1 bill; it is the $100 bill.)

(g) The letter "o" (or nothing).

(h) There is no such thing as a mommy bull.

(i) His undertaker.

(j) It is very likely. The average number of arms is very slightly less than two, so anyone with two arms has more than the average.

(k) Guilty but in Seine.

(l) Two. One on each side.

(m) All 12 of them.

(n) Pigs cannot say.

(o) Eleven, just as before (the tide also raises the boat).

35

4.17 Healthy People I

In the early twentieth century many healthy people were operated on for medical conditions they did not have. Why?

4.18 Healthy People II

A hospital director recently confirmed that many of the people admitted to his hospital were not ill at all. They were perfectly healthy, yet they were given hospital care and treatment. Why?

4.19 The Grand Prix

A world-famous racing driver was approaching a bend in a formula-one Grand Prix race. Suddenly he braked very sharply and came around the bend to find crashed cars strewn dangerously across the track. He had not been able to see over or around the bend. The officials had not warned him and there was no smoke, fire, smell, or noise that he could have detected. So how did he know that something was wrong in time to avoid danger?

4.20 The Stranger in the Car

A man and his wife were driving quickly from the suburbs into town when their car ran out of fuel. The man left his wife in the car after telling her to keep the windows closed and the doors locked. When he returned, although the doors and windows were still locked and had remained so throughout, he found his wife dead inside and a stranger in the car. The car had not been broken into or damaged in any way, and it had no sun-roof or hatchback; the only means of entry were the doors. How had the wife died and who was the stranger?

4.21 Eggshell Finish

Why was the man painting his portrait on an eggshell?

THE CLUES

1 Easy Puzzles

1.1 The Apple Problem

Q: Were any of the apples split or eaten?
A: No.

Q: Did each of the six girls get one apple?
A: Yes.

Q: Were there only six girls and no other people in the room?
A: Yes.

Q: Were there only six apples in the room both at the beginning and end of the process?
A: Yes.

Q: Did any girl get more than one apple?
A: Yes.

1.2 The Two Presidents

Q: Were they brother and sister?
A: No. (There has not yet been a woman president.)

Q: Were they both elected through the normal electoral process?
A: Yes.

Q: Were they both men?
A: Yes.

1.3 Game, Set, and Match

Q: Were they playing standard regulation tennis?
A: Yes.

Q: Were they both physically normal?
A: Yes.

Q: Were they playing on the same court at the same time?
A: Yes.

1.4 Wondrous Walk

Q: Was it a very short distance that he walked?
A: No. He walked from Dublin to Cork and that is nearly two hundred miles.

Q: Are there many pubs on the road from Dublin to Cork?
A: Yes.

Q: Did he take a particular route to avoid the pubs?
A: No.

Q: Did he use special roads such as turnpikes, highways, tunnels, newly constructed roads, etc.?
A: No. He used the normal roads.

Q: Did it take him a long time to complete the journey?
A: Yes, very.

1.5   Father and Son

It is impossible for a father to be younger than his son. However, it is possible to have a grandfather who is younger than your father. Alternatively, you could have a grandmother younger than your mother. However, it is not possible to have a grandfather *and* grandmother younger than your father and mother. Confused? Keep thinking!

1.6   The Amazing Fall

Q: Did he wear any special clothing or glider wings?
A: No.

Q: Was he a normal man?
A: Yes.

Q: Did he come in contact with anything on the way down which slowed his fall?
A: No. He fell from the plane to the ground and accelerated all the way.

Q: How high was the plane?
A: It was 5,000 feet above sea level (but it was not flying over the sea).

Q: Was the plane flying fast?
A: No.

1.7   Shopping Is Good for You

Q: Did he need to buy some drug or medication?
A: No.

Q: Was he fully conscious and awake when he crashed the plane?
A: Yes.

Q: Did he deliberately ignore his tutor's instructions?
A: No.

Q: Did he deliberately crash the plane?
A: No.

Q: Did he have some kind of ailment or disability?
A: Yes.

1.8 Your Turn to Drive

Q: Were both brothers able and licensed to drive?
A: Yes.

Q: Did one always drive in Birmingham and the other in London?
A: Yes.

Q: Was this through choice or necessity?
A: Necessity, they did not like this.

Q: When one drove was his brother a passenger?
A: Yes.

Q: Do their jobs have any relevance?
A: No.

Q: Do the cities have relevance?
A: Yes.

Q: Were the brothers normal in every way?
A: No.

1.9 See Saw

There is no hidden catch in this. What is the easiest and most direct way for this man to communicate his request?

1.10 The Two Lookouts

Q: Were the two lookouts facing in opposite directions?
A: Yes.

Q: Were any mirrors, lenses, or cameras involved?
A: No.

Q: Could each see the other's face?
A: Yes.

1.11 The Deadly Drive

Q: Was anything mechanical or electrical in his car tampered with?
A: No.

Q: Was his death an accident?
A: Yes.

Q: Was something stolen which could have prevented this accident?
A: Yes.

Q: Was it something he used while driving?
A: Yes.

1.12   Another Man in an Elevator

Q: Is he completely capable of operating the elevator?
A: Yes.

Q: If he wanted to go up to his room at some other time of day would he use the elevator?
A: Yes.

Q: Do other guests use the elevator to ascend in the evening?
A: Yes.

Q: Is the man physically normal?
A: Yes.

Q: Is he alone on his journey at eight every evening?
A: No.

Q: Does this regular evening journey serve a useful purpose?
A: Yes.

1.13   Growing Younger

Q: Was Ben a normal human being?
A: Yes.

Q: Was he born on February 29?
A: No.

Q: As each year went by did he get one year older?
A: Yes.

Q: Does it have something to do with the dates?
A: Yes.

1.14 The Habitual Walker

Q: Was the train a special train of some kind?
A: No. It was the regular train.

Q: Was the train early?
A: No.

Q: Is his deafness relevant?
A: Yes, but only because he could not hear train coming.

Q: Had his clock stopped?
A: No, he had three clocks and wound them all the night before. They all kept good time.

Q: Was there something special about that particular day which threw out his schedule?
A: Yes.

1.15 Greenland

Q: Was the country green when he discovered it?
A: No.

Q: Did he believe that it would or could become green?
A: No.

Q: Did he name it after some person or place?
A: No.

Q: Was the name given meant to be descriptive?
A: Yes.

Q: Was the name in any way accurate?
A: No.

1.16 Radio On

Q: Did the girl influence or direct the radio in any way?
A: No.

Q: Did everyone listening to that station at the time suffer the same loss of reception?
A: No. Most did not but a small number did.

Q: Was it anything to do with her location?
A: Yes.

Q: Is this a rare or a common occurrence?
A: Common.

1.17 The Boxing Match

Q: Did one boxer kick or butt the other boxer, or hit him with some implement?
A: No.

Q: Was everything about the fight legal and proper?
A: Yes.

Q: And yet no punches were thrown?
A: No man threw a punch.

Q: Was there something unusual about the two boxers?
A: Yes.

1.18 The Nephew

There is no catch to this one. The man and woman were a normal brother and sister. The boy was the man's nephew but he was not the woman's nephew. There is a very simple explanation.

1.19 Barrel Trouble

When he started, the barrel was empty. He then filled it with something. That something was not a light gas nor was it anything lighter than air. There are no vacuums or tricky physics involved. Anyone could do this!

1.20 Rival Fans

Q: Did they know each other?
A: No.

Q: Was the Argentinian fan grateful to the man who had struck him?
A: Yes.

Q: Did the Brazilian fan help his rival in some way?
A: Yes.

1.21 Coming Up for Air

Q: Could she get a valid sample by simply taking the lid off the jar and shaking it around?
A: No. How could she be sure that she had removed all the original air?

Q: Did she use some kind of machine to create a vacuum?
A: No.

Q: Does the solution involve advanced physics or complicated devices?
A: No. She used a very simple idea.

1.22 Nuts Away!

Q: Did the boy suggest a way of attaching the wheel?
A: Yes.

Q: Did it involve retrieving the lost nuts?
A: No.

Q: Did it involve any equipment not normally available in a car?
A: No.

Q: Was it a sensible idea which was easy to implement?
A: Yes.

1.23 The Golf Pro

Q: Does this have anything to do with a left-hander's golf clubs or equipment or methods?
A: No.

Q: Is it because left-handed players make better teachers?
A: Yes. Why?

1.24 Deduction

Q: Did the man find the name and address written down somewhere?

A: No.

Q: Did he follow his wife or have her followed?

A: No.

Q: Did he find some article giving a clue to the lover's identity?

A: No.

Q: Was he expecting to find her on his return?

A: No. He thought that she would arrange to meet her lover.

2 Moderate Puzzles

2.1 The Penny Black

Q: Was the paper or the ink of the Penny Black defective in any way?

A: No.

Q: Did the design change when the Penny Red was introduced?

A: No, only the color.

Q: Was there a problem with the Penny Black because it was black?

A: Yes.

Q: Did the problem have to do with the printing or copying?

A: No.

2.2 Flat Tire I

Q: Did he drive all those miles with a flat tire?

A: Yes.

Q: Did it make steering or braking or balancing the car more difficult?
A: No.

Q: Did he do something to the flat tire or to any of the other tires or wheels?
A: No.

Q: Did he drive on the wheel rim?
A: No.

Q: Did he have a special car or special skill?
A: No. Anyone could do this in any car.

2.3 Flat Tire II

The instructor could not tell from their clothing or the weather or any other external factor whether they were telling the truth. The tardy students had in fact arrived by car but had suffered no puncture or flat tire. The lecturer asked them one question which exposed their deceit. What was the question?

2.4 Bottled Fruit

This is not only physically possible; it is often done. There are producers who sell a fully grown pear inside each bottle of pear liqueur. The mouth of the bottle is much smaller than the pear, yet they get the pear into the bottle without any special implements or aids and they do not form the bottle around the pear. How do they do it?

2.5 The Cowboy's Fate

Q: Was this cause of death accidental?
A: Yes.

Q: Did it involve firearms?
A: No.

Q: Did it involve other people?
A: No.

Q: Did it involve animals?
A: Yes.

Q: Did these animals attack them?
A: No.

2.6 The Village Idiot

Q: Was the village idiot simply an idiot?
A: No.

Q: Was there a good reason for him to always choose the coin rather than the bill?
A: Yes.

Q: Was getting the money in coin in some way more valuable or useful to him than having a bill would be?
A: No.

2.7   The Island Fire

Q: Does the solution involve him going into the sea or using sea water?
A: No. There were steep cliffs plunging into shark-infested seas!

Q: Does he have time to cut a fire-break?
A: No.

Q: Can he use something to put out the fire?
A: No.

Q: Does he stay on the island the whole time?
A: Yes.

Q: Is the strong wind relevant?
A: Yes.

2.8   The Sleepy Kings

Q: Were the two kings related in any way?
A: No.

Q: Were the kings both physically normal?
A: Yes.

Q: Did these events happen about the same time?
A: No. King George II's "long sleep" took place in 1752, some 170 years after the similar episode for King Henry III.

Q: Were they suffering from some illness or using some kind of drug?
A: No.

Q: Did it matter that they were kings?
A: No.

Q: Was this a normal occurrence at that time?
A: Yes.

2.9   The Portrait

Do not make any assumptions here. Work through the statements logically. Start at the end—if he has no brothers then who can "my father's son" be?

2.10   Winning Isn't Everything

Q: Is there some trick about stroke play/match play or not finishing particular games?
A: No.

Q: Is there something particular to golf or could they have played any sport where they finish 1, 2, 3?
A: Any sport.

Q: Were they correct in their calculations?
A: Yes.

Q: Did each of them win about the same number of games?
A: Yes.

2.11   The Reluctant Diner

Q: Was he trying to lose weight?
A: No.

Q: Had he planned to eat with someone else?
A: No.

Q: Was he able to eat before 8 P.M.?
A: Yes.

Q: Is there a medical or social reason for his reluctance to eat?
A: No.

Q: Was he thirsty and did he drink before 8 P.M.?
A: He was thirsty but he did not drink.

(BONUS CLUE: The next evening he did the same thing but waited until two minutes past eight before eating and drinking.)

2.12   Death in a Car

Q: Was his death murder or suicide?
A: No, it was an accident.

Q: Was he or the car unusual in any way?
A: No.

Q: Did he know he was going to die?
A: Yes, but only just before he died.

Q: Was the car in a moving accident?
A: No. It was stationary immediately before, during, and after his death.

Q: Was there any wound or mark on his body?
A: No.

Q: Was any other person or animal involved?
A: No.

Q: Was the location where he parked the car critical?
A: Yes.

2.13   Last Cord

Q: Was he strangled by the cord?
A: No.

Q: Was his death an accident?
A: Yes.

Q: Did any other human or animal cause his death?
A: No.

Q: Was his death violent?
A: Yes.

Q: Was it a special kind of cord?
A: Yes, and it was broken.

2.14   Saturday Flights

Q: Does it involve time zones or calendar changes?
A: No.

Q: Did he spend just 4 nights and 5 days in Los Angeles?
A: Yes.

Q: Did he arrive and leave by plane?
A: Yes.

Q: Was it a scheduled flight or a private plane?
A: A private plane.

2.15   The Trains That Did Not Crash

Q: Did each train run from one end of the tunnel through and out the opposite end?
A: Yes.

Q: Did both trains run on the same single track but in opposite directions?
A: Yes.

Q: Were they normal, full-sized trains?
A: Yes.

Q: Did they somehow pass by each other in the tunnel?
A: No.

2.16   Copyright

It is impossible to have a copyright restriction on the words of the English language or the shape of the continents of the world. But it is possible to copyright specific expressions of these concepts, as in a proprietary dictionary or atlas. How would you know if someone had copied your specific list of words or representation of the world and claimed it to be an original work? How could you prove the person had copied your expression rather than come up with the work independently?

2.17   The Ransom

Q: Did the man receive a phone call at the phone booth?
A: No.

Q: Was the kidnapper in the park?
A: No.

Q: Did the kidnapper get the diamond safely out of the park?
A: Yes.

Q: Was any other person involved?
A: No.

Q: Did the diamond leave the park in some sort of vehicle or through a tunnel?
A: No.

2.18 Moving Parts

Q: Do both objects serve a common and useful function?
A: Yes.

Q: Does either of them use electricity?
A: No.

Q: Are the thousands of moving parts man-made?
A: No.

Q: Are the objects recent inventions?
A: No. They have both been around in one form or another for centuries.

Q: Are they in common use indoors?
A: The one with thousands of parts is commonly found indoors. The other is not in such common use and is found outdoors.

2.19 An Early Burial

Q: Was he buried the same week of the same year?
A: Yes.

Q: Was he buried the day before he died?
A: Yes.

Q: Was he dead when he was buried?
A: Yes.

Q: Does where he died and was buried have anything to do with it?
A: Yes.

Q: Could this happen in, say, New York or London?
A: No.

2.20   Trouble and Strife

Q: Was she angry because of who called or what the caller said?
A: No.

Q: Did either of them know the caller?
A: No.

Q: Was she angry because of what her husband said?
A: Yes.

Q: Did he hold a long conversation with the caller?
A: No. He answered the phone in the normal way and replaced the receiver when he learned that it was a wrong number.

Q: Did she have good reason to be upset?
A: Yes.

Q: If she had not been knitting would she have been angry?
A: No.

2.21   Bath Water

Q: Was the maid heating water on the stove in order to add all of it to the bath water?
A: Yes.

Q: Was the temperature in the house steady?
A: Yes.

Q: Was there anything unusual about the kitchen, the stove, the water, or the bathtub?
A: No.

Q: Was the water very hot?
A: Yes. It was steaming.

2.22 The Hold-Up

Q: Were the people whom the man held up angry?
A: Yes.

Q: Was the policeman an accomplice?
A: No. He was a regular policeman.

Q: Did he know the man?
A: No.

Q: Did the policeman clearly see and understand the man's wrongdoing?
A: Yes.

Q: Did the policeman try to take back the $200?
A: Certainly not! But he did tell the man not to hold up people again.

2.23 The Worst Sailor

Q: Did Jim have some special skill or attribute useful to the captain?
A: No.

Q: Did he perform some other tasks?
A: No. He was just one of the sailors.

Q: Was he less expensive to pay or keep than the other sailors?
A: No.

Q: Was the ship a real ship at sea?
A: Yes.

2.24 The Valuable Book

Q: Did he destroy the book because it contained something damaging or threatening to him or his family?
A: No.

Q: Was he hoping to collect the insurance?
A: No.

Q: Does this involve fraud, blackmail, or robbery?
A: No.

Q: Was he breaking the law by burning this book?
A: No.

Q: Did he do it for personal gain?
A: Yes.

3 Difficult Puzzles

3.1 Cuddly Bears

Q: Did the hospital lock up or guard the bears?
A: No.

Q: Did they make them deliberately unattractive to the children?
A: No.

Q: Did they threaten or penalize the children or their parents?
A: No.

Q: Did they play on the children's love and concern for the bears?

3.2 The High-Society Dinner

Q: Was the man a thief or the thief's accomplice?
A: No.

Q: Did he have a coin in his pocket?
A: No.

Q: Was he an aristocrat like the other guests?
A: Yes.

Q: Was he afraid of showing what was in his pockets?
A: Yes.

Q: Would it show that he was a criminal?
A: No.

Q: Had he taken something?
A: Yes.

3.3 Eight Years Old

Q: Was the girl physically normal?
A: Yes.

Q: Were her eight years normal earth years of twelve months each?
A: Yes.

Q: Was she sixteen on her second birthday?
A: No.

Q: Was she nine on her second birthday?
A: No.

Q: Could she have been born this century?
A: No. Though she did live this century.

Q: Was she unique in being eight years old on her first birthday?
A: No. It happened to everyone else born when she was born.

3.4 Cover That Hole

Q: Was it something peculiar to the town?
A: No. It would be a good idea anywhere.

Q: Does it have to do with cost or efficiency?
A: No.

Q: Does it have to do with safety?
A: Yes.

Q: Are manhole covers the same shape but slightly larger than the manhole rims?
A: Yes.

3.5 The Protagoras Paradox

In approaching the trial each man felt that he had an excellent chance of winning. The young man argued that if he won his case the court would have cleared him of any obligation to pay. If he lost the case he would still not have won his first case and would therefore still be free of the obligations of the original contract.

Protagoras believed that if he won the case, it meant by definition that the court had found in his favor against his former pupil, who would therefore have to pay him any specified damages, i.e., the tuition fees. On the other hand if he lost his case, then his opponent, the pupil, would have won his first case and would therefore be contractually bound to pay.

3.6 Hand in Glove

Q: Did the glove manufacturer smuggle the gloves into the country?
A: No! He was a reputable businessman.

Q: Did he disguise them as something else?
A: No.

Q: Did he pay any duty?
A: No.

Q: Are your goods impounded if you refuse to pay duty?
A: Yes, the goods are then sold at auction to the highest bidder. (The value of the sets of gloves at auction would be higher than the duty.)

3.7   The School Superintendent

Q: Did the superintendent ask plenty of questions?
A: Yes.

Q: Did all the children raise their hands?
A: Yes.

Q: Did the teacher always pick a child who knew the answer?
A: Yes.

Q: Were they normal children?
A: Yes.
Q: Did all the children know all the answers?
A: No.

Q: Did the teacher know the questions in advance?
A: No.

3.8 No Trumps

There are four separate hands at bridge; each with 13 cards. The 13 trumps are randomly distributed between the four hands. It would be terrific if you and your partner had all 13 trumps as you would be bound to win at least seven tricks. It is unlikely that you would have all 13 trumps; but is it even more unlikely that you will have none between you?

3.9 How to Beat Nick Faldo

Q: Did they play a game of golf on a proper golf course?
A: Yes.

Q: Was the challenger also a world-class player?
A: No. He was a good player.

Q: Did the champion play his best?
A: Yes.

Q: Did the timing of the match give the challenger his advantage?
A: Yes.

3.10 How to Beat Carl Lewis

Q: Did they run a race?
A: Yes.

Q: Was the time they ran the race important?
A: No.

Q: Did they run backwards, sideways, or on their hands?
A: No.

Q: Was it a long-distance race?
A: No, it covered a short distance.

3.11 The Missing Furniture

Q: Did he fall to his death?
A: No.

Q: Was his death an accident?
A: Yes.

Q: Was the piece of furniture heavy or unusual?
A: No. It was a very common piece of furniture.

Q: Was his job unusual and dangerous?
A: Yes.

3.12 The Dead Man

Q: Was the cord attached to anything else in the room before or during his death?
A: No.

Q: Was any ice involved?
A: No. (What an odd question!)

Q: Was his death a suicide?
A: Yes.

Q: Was any other person or thing involved?
A: No.

3.13 The Busy Hospital

Q: Did people drive faster or more dangerously because they wore seat belts?
A: No.

Q: Was there an increase in injuries to pedestrians, cyclists, or other road users?
A: No, but there were more injured drivers and passengers.

Q: Was the seriousness of the injuries generally reduced?
A: Yes.

Q: Was there something peculiar about this town, its inhabitants, or the hospital?
A: No.

Q: Was the wearing of seat belts successful in its aim of improving road safety?
A: Yes.

3.14   The Fallen Sign

Q: Could the man see the correct position by matching the broken parts of the post or the post with the hole in the ground?
A: No.

Q: Did he use the sun, stars, wind, or a landmark as a guide?
A: No.

Q: Did he use some piece of knowledge to replace the sign correctly in the ground?
A: Yes.

Q: Could anyone have done this or did he have some special skill or knowledge?
A: Anyone could have done it.

3.15   False Fingerprints

Q: Did the man use his wife's fingerprints?
A: No.

Q: Had he brought in a set of false fingerprints especially for this purpose?
A: No. He thought of doing it on the spur of the moment.

Q: Did he have some particular skill or knowledge of science to plant the false prints?
A: No.

Q: Did he use something easily available?
A: Yes.

Q: Did it fool the police?
A: Yes.

Q: Did he leave a proper set of fingerprints on the murder weapon?
A: No.

3.16   Found, Lost, Found

Q: Did the man deliberately throw away something which he valued?
A: Yes.

Q: Was he pleased to throw it away?
A: Yes.

Q: Was he later pleased to get it back?
A: Yes.

Q: Did he simply change his mind?
A: No. The circumstances changed.

Q: When he threw it away, did it represent a danger?
A: Yes.

Q: Did it present a danger when he got it back?
A: No.

3.17   The Crippled Child

Q: Did the parents believe that the child would eventually be cured?
A: No, they understood it was permanently disabled.

Q: Were they sadistic or malevolent in some way?
A: No.

Q: Was the child's handicap of some use to them?
A: Yes, quite beneficial in fact.

64

Q: Does this usefulness involve medical research or religion?
A: No.

3.18 Insurance

Q: Was this an unusual ambition?
A: No. Many people share this personal goal.

Q: Would achieving this goal injure or kill him?
A: No.

Q: Was it a dangerous undertaking to him or to others?
A: No.

Q: Was it something which would prove costly?
A: Yes.

Q: Is it something which involves skill or luck?
A: Yes, both.

3.19 Eggs

The reason has to do with a practical advantage for the survival of the birds. It is based on a simple physical consequence of the shape. It has nothing to do with the act of egg laying.

3.20 The Guard Dog

Q: Did the boy enter the orchard while the dog was there?
A: Yes.

Q: Did he drug the dog or trap it?
A: No. It remained free to move around.

Q: Did he give it food?
A: No.

Q: Did he distract it in some way?
A: Yes.

3.21 The Last Message

Q: Had the man been murdered and the scene made to look like suicide?
A: Yes.

Q: Was there something about the room or the desk or the gun which indicated to the detective that it was murder?
A: No.

Q: Was the clue in the cassette recording?
A: Yes.

Q: Did it have to do with the man's voice or accent?
A: No.

3.22 The Japanese Speaker

Q: Was it the fact that an American was speaking Japanese which amused them?
A: No.

Q: Was it the subject matter?
A: No.

Q: Was it the way he spoke?
A: Yes.

Q: Was it his American accent or his grammar?
A: No.

Q: Was he taught by a good Japanese speaker?
A: Yes. He was taught by his wife, who was Japanese.

4   Fiendish Puzzles

4.1 The Cellar Door

Q: Did the little girl see something which amazed or surprised her?
A: Yes.

Q: Would it amaze or surprise most people?
A: No.

Q: Was something unusual kept in the cellar?
A: Yes.

Q: Is this what she saw?
A: No.

Q: Did she see a living creature?
A: No.

4.2   The Deadly Shot

Q: Does it matter what the man shot at?
A: No.

Q: Did he hit what he shot at?
A: Irrelevant.

Q: Was any other human or animal involved in his death?
A: No.

Q: Did something fall on him out of the sky?
A: No.

Q: Did he know he was going to die before he died?
A: Yes.

Q: Did he know he was going to die before he fired the gun?
A: No.

4.3   Flat Out

Q: Were the road and railway track at right angles to each other and did they cross on the same ground?
A: Yes.

Q: Did the driver go over a bridge or under a tunnel?
A: No.

Q: Did the car, the driver, and the train all get across the level crossing intact?
A: Yes.

Q: Were the car and the train on the level crossing at the exact same instant?
A: Yes.

4.4 An Odd Story

This puzzle does not involve putting one cup inside another cup or transferring coffee or sugar from one cup to another. Nor does it involve one man drinking another man's coffee. How could each man put an odd number of lumps in his drink yet exactly 12 lumps (an even number) were used altogether?

4.5 Free Maps

Q: Did the British government sell the maps to cover the costs?
A: No.

Q: Did they get the use of the planes, photographers, and other needs free?
A: No.

Q: Were the maps produced accurate?
A: Yes.

Q: Did they reveal useful or unexpected information?
A: Yes.

Q: Did the government sell this information?
A: No.

Q: Did they raise money because they now had this information?
A: Yes.

4.6 What a Shock I

Q: Did the man see something or someone?
A: Someone.

Q: Was the person he saw alive?
A: No.

Q: Did he expect to see someone else?
A: Yes.

Q: Did he now know that he would soon die?
A: Yes.

4.7 What a Shock II

Q: Did the man see a dead human or animal?
A: No.

Q: Did he see objects which terrified him?
A: Yes.

Q: What were they?
A: Glass eyes!

Q: Did seeing them make him realize that he would soon die?
A: Yes.

4.8 The Deadly Party

Q: Did the man poison the other people?
A: No.

Q: Did anybody add anything to the punch after he left?
A: No.

Q: Was there something wrong with the glasses, ladle, or the punch bowl itself?
A: No.

Q: Were all the people physically normal?
A: Yes.

Q: Was there a relationship between the people, or between them and the man who left early, that matters here?
A: No.

Q: Was there something special about him which made him immune to the poison?
A: No. It could have been anyone, provided they left early.

4.9 Speechless

Q: Did the two friends recognize and greet each other?
A: Yes.

Q: Were they close to each other?
A: Yes.

Q: Were they being watched or supervised?
A: No.

Q: Were they afraid of being overheard?
A: No.

Q: Could other people there speak?
A: No.

Q: Was it indoors?
A: No.

4.10 How to Hug

Q: Was the book about hugging or embracing?
A: No.

Q: Did it have the wrong cover or a misprinted cover?
A: No.

Q: Was it a genuine non-fiction book written in English?
A: Yes.

Q: Was the boy physically normal and could he read?
A: Yes.

Q: Was the title of the book an accurate description of its contents?
A: Yes.

Q: Would one recognize this type of book if one saw it?
A: Yes.

4.11 The Healthy Dairymaids

Q: Were other sections of the community immune from smallpox or was it just dairymaids?
A: Just dairymaids.

Q: Was it something to do with drinking milk or eating dairy produce?
A: No.

Q: Was it because of the way the dairymaids milked the cows?
A: No.

Q: Did they gain an immunity because they worked closely with cows?
A: Yes.

Q: Were they immune because they had previously caught smallpox?
A: No.

4.12 Toothache

This story is based on fact. It happened to a man in Sweden at around the turn of the century. It is extremely unlikely that it could happen nowadays. The man had been poor but at the time of the trial he was wealthy. He was physically and mentally normal, and was not a criminal. The teeth he had had removed were normal human teeth with no particular value. However, he was judged to have injured the interests of a third party by having those teeth out. Why?

4.13 The Lake Problem

Q: Does the solution involve measuring the height of the water in the lake?
A: No.

Q: Does the solution involve measuring the temperature of the lake?
A: No.

Q: Is the solution a practical and realistic way of estimating the volume of water in the lake?
A: Yes.

Q: Does the solution involve taking samples of water from the lake?
A: Yes.

4.14 The Realization

Q: Had the man's wife died?
A: Yes.

Q: Was it murder, an accident, or suicide?
A: It was an accident.

Q: Was she in the same building as he was?
A: Yes, but she was on another floor—well outside his sight and hearing range.

Q: Did he hear something?
A: No.

Q: Did he see something which caused him to realize she had died?
A: Yes.

Q: Was it something major like a fire or explosion which killed her?
A: No. Other people near her did not die.

4.15 The Deadly Dish

Q: Was the dish poisoned or distasteful in some way?
A: It was not poisoned. It was not distasteful to anyone but him.

Q: Did tasting the dish cause him to deliberately commit suicide?
A: Yes.

Q: Did he recognize the taste?
A: No, but that was the reason that he shot himself.

Q: Was the dish human flesh, or the flesh of a pet or an endangered species?
A: No. It was the meat of a bird.

Q: Was there something in his earlier life which was linked to his recognizing or not recognizing the taste?
A: Yes.

4.16 Men in Uniform

Q: Were the two men both wearing the same uniform?
A: No.

Q: Had the angry man killed the other man?
A: Yes.

Q: Was it an accident or a case of mistaken identity?
A: No.

Q: Was something preventing the murderer from leaving the scene?
A: Yes.

4.17 Healthy People I

Q: Did this actually happen?
A: Yes.

Q: Were the people unusual in any way? Were they of one particular race or type or sex?
A: No.

Q: Were their operations genuine mistakes on the part of the medical community?
A: Yes.

Q: Were they wrongly diagnosed because of the use of some new technology or medical method?
A: Yes.

Q: Is it a technology or method which is in common use today?
A: Yes.

4.18 Healthy People II

Q: Is this occurrence unusual?
A: No. It is common.

Q: Are these people mentally ill or socially deprived?
A: No.

Q: Does their physical state require hospital treatment?
A: Strictly speaking, no, but it is usual and beneficial.

4.19 The Grand Prix

Q: Was there a car ahead of him which swerved?
A: No.

Q: Did he know for sure there was a crash around the bend?
A: No, but he knew that something was happening there.

Q: Did he see something which alerted him?
A: Yes.

Q: Was it a deliberate signal from someone or something?
A: No.

4.20   The Stranger in the Car

Q: Was there something special or unusual about the car?
A: No. It was a regular four-door family car.

Q: Was the stranger a human being? Which sex?
A: Yes. Male.

Q: Was the woman's death murder or suicide?
A: No. It was accidental.

Q: Did she die of poisoning, suffocation, or heart attack?
A: No.

Q: Was the stranger the cause of the woman's death?
A: Yes, although not deliberately.

4.21   Eggshell Finish

Q: Was the man a serious painter?
A: No.

Q: Was he painting his likeness on the eggshell for fun?
A: No, he had a very good reason.

Q: Does his profession matter?
A: Yes.

Q: Did the portrait really look like him?
A: Yes, when he was working.

THE ANSWERS

1 Easy Puzzles

1.1 The Apple Problem

The first five girls each took an apple. The sixth girl took the basket as well as the apple in it.

1.2 The Two Presidents

They were the same man. Grover Cleveland (1837–1908) served two terms as president of the United States, but the terms were not consecutive. He was president from 1885 to 1889 and from 1893 to 1897.

1.3 Game, Set, and Match

The two men were partners playing doubles.

1.4 Wondrous Walk

The man did not pass a single pub because he went into every one!

1.5 Father and Son

Let's say that William's father was 60, his mother was 25, and his mother's father was 45. Because everyone has two grandfathers, it is quite possible for a maternal grandfather to be younger than one's father.

1.6 The Amazing Fall

The plane was parked on the runway.

1.7 Shopping Is Good for You

The man had neglected to buy a new battery for his hearing aid. The old battery failed just as he was coming in to land and he therefore did not hear his tutor's crucial instructions.

1.8 Your Turn to Drive

The brothers were Siamese twins, joined at the side. They lived in Birmingham, Alabama. Because they drove on the right-hand side of the road the steering wheel was on the left-hand side of the car. The brother who sat on the left always drove. When they were in London, England, the other drove because the steering wheel was on the right-hand side of the car.

1.9 See Saw

The deaf man says to the storekeeper, "I would like to buy a saw, please."

1.10 The Two Lookouts

Although the guards were looking in opposite directions, they were not back to back. They were facing each other.

1.11 The Deadly Drive

The man's expensive designer sunglasses were stolen. He normally wore them while driving. As he came around a bend in the mountain, he was blinded by the evening sun and ran off the road.

1.12 Another Man in an Elevator

Bill was on holiday with his wife and two-year-old son. The boy is a very lively fellow. Bill and his wife found that the best way to tire the youngster out each night was to let him climb five flights of stairs just before his bedtime. He enjoyed doing it but for Bill it was a chore.

1.13   Growing Younger

Ben was born in the year 2000 B.C. So in 1985 B.C. he was 15 and in 1980 B.C. he was 20.

1.14   The Habitual Walker

On that particular morning all the clocks were due to be moved forward for the summer. Although he had wound all his clocks he had neglected to put them forward one hour. Consequently, when he set out thinking it was 7:45 A.M. it was really 8:45 A.M. He was hit by the 9 o'clock train.

1.15   Greenland

In about 982 a Norseman, Eric the Red, discovered Greenland. He wanted to encourage people to settle there so he called it Greenland to make it sound attractive. It is a very early example of deliberately misleading labelling!

1.16   Radio On

The girl was listening to the radio in her father's car. He drove through a tunnel and reception was temporarily interrupted.

1.17   The Boxing Match

No man threw a punch because the boxing match was between two women boxers.

1.18   The Nephew

The boy was the woman's son, and therefore he was her brother's nephew.

1.19   Barrel Trouble

The man filled the barrel with holes! Since there was now less barrel it weighed less.

78

1.20 Rival Fans

The two men were in a restaurant. The Argentinian fan had a fishbone stuck in his throat and was choking. The other man was quick-witted enough to give him a strong blow on the back, thereby dislodging the bone and saving his life.

1.21 Coming Up for Air

The girl filled the jar with water at the school. When she reached the appropriate point at the city center she poured all the water out. What replaced it was a true sample of the surrounding air.

1.22 Nuts Away!

The boy suggested that the man take one wheel nut off each of the other three wheels in order to attach the fourth wheel. Once he had done this, the man could safely drive to the nearest garage with each wheel firmly attached by three nuts.

1.23 The Golf Pro

One of the most important tasks for the golf club professional is giving lessons. Most players are right-handed. They can stand opposite a left-handed teacher and watch and copy him more easily. It is just like looking in a mirror, so it makes learning the correct style of swing easier.

1.24 Deduction

He reasoned that she would have called her lover so he simply pressed the redial button on their telephone. When the man answered with his name the husband told him that he had won a prize draw and asked for the address to which it should be sent.

2 Moderate Puzzles

2.1 The Penny Black

The postmark used at that time was always black. It was therefore difficult to tell whether a stamp had been franked or not. This led to people reusing used stamps. On a Penny Red the black postmark was clearly visible.

2.2 Flat Tire I

The flat tire was on the man's spare wheel which he kept in the car trunk. The four wheels he drove on all had properly inflated tires.

2.3 Flat Tire II

The lecturer separated the four students, so that they were not together in the room, and asked each to write down which of the four wheels of the car had suffered the puncture. Of course they did not all say the same wheel. (The chances of them all picking the same wheel are 1 in $4 \times 4 \times 4$; i.e., 1 in 64.)

2.4 Bottled Fruit

The fruit is grown in the bottle. The bottle is tied onto the branch shortly after the fruit starts to form.

2.5 The Cowboy's Fate

The most common cause of death among cowboys was from being dragged along by a galloping horse when the cowboy's foot was caught in a stirrup. This would occur during a fall or when mounting or dismounting.

2.6 The Village Idiot

The so-called village idiot was smart enough to realize that as long as he kept choosing the 50-cent piece, people would keep offering him the choice. If he once took the $5 bill, the stream of coins would stop rolling in.

2.7 The Island Fire

The man should set fire to the ground beneath him and walk towards the main fire. The wind will fan the fire he started so as to burn out the end of the island towards which the wind is blowing. He can then walk back to a piece of burnt land and stand there safely when the main fire reaches his end of the island.

2.8 The Sleepy Kings

The kings each slept one night only. The calendar changed in France in 1582 and in England in 1752. Previously the Julian Calendar had been used, but this had allowed a cumulative error to occur which needed to be corrected. Pope Gregory XIII ordered ten days to be dropped from the year 1582. This order was followed by Catholic countries such as France but not by Protestant ones such as England. England eventually adopted the improved Gregorian Calendar in 1752, though by that time the adjustment needed had grown to 11 days.

Incidentally, the thirteen American colonies were under British control so they also changed from Julian to Gregorian calendars in 1752. George Washington was born on February 11, 1732, but after 1752 his birthday became February 22, which is now officially Washington's Birthday.

2.9 The Portrait

The portrait is of the man's daughter.

2.10 Winning Isn't Everything

One third of the games finished A, B, C; one third finished B, C, A, and the other third finished C, A, B. So Alf finished ahead of Bert twice as often as behind him and the same is true for Bert over Chris and Chris over Alf.

2.11 The Reluctant Diner

The businessman was a Muslim. He therefore observed the religious fast for the month of Ramadan. During this period Muslims are not allowed to drink, eat, or smoke between sunrise and sunset.

2.12 Death in a Car

The man drove his car to the beach to watch the sunset over the waves. He fell asleep. The tide came in and seeped in around the car doors and windows. He awoke, but with the pressure of the water, he couldn't get out of the car. The water filled the car and drowned him. Later the tide went out and he was found dead in an empty car.

2.13 Last Cord

Incredible as it may seem, some people enjoy leaping off high buildings or bridges with a length of elastic cord fastened to them. This pastime is known as bungee jumping. The poor man in this situation died when he jumped from a high crane in the field and his bungee cord broke.

2.14 Saturday Flights

Saturday was the name of the man's private plane.

2.15 The Trains That Did Not Crash

One train went through the tunnel in the early afternoon and the other went through in the late afternoon.

2.16 Copyright

Publishers normally include a nonexistent word or a nonexistent island in a dictionary or atlas, respectively. If it then appears in somebody else's work, they have clear evidence of copying.

2.17 The Ransom

This is a true story from Taiwan. When the rich man reached the phone booth he found a carrier pigeon in a cage. It had a message attached telling the man to put the diamond in a small bag which was around the pigeon's neck and to release the bird. When the man did this the police were powerless to follow the bird as it returned across the city to its owner.

2.18   Moving Parts

The two objects are an hourglass (often used in the kitchen as an egg-timer) and a sundial.

2.19   An Early Burial

John Brown lived on a Pacific island close to the International Date Line. When you cross the International Date Line (eastwards), your calendar goes back one day. He died on Thursday, December 6, and was flown home that same day for burial. Because the plane flew eastwards over the International Date Line it was Wednesday, December 5, when he was buried later that day. (This could happen if the plane flew, for example, from Fiji to Western Samoa.)

2.20   Trouble and Strife

Mrs. White had been counting her stitches very carefully; the number was well past 300. When Mr. White answered the phone he told the caller their phone number, 837-9263. Hearing this caused Mrs. White to lose count.

2.21   Bath Water

The water in the pan was already boiling when the butler came in. The longer the maid now heated the water the less of it there would be (because of the steam) to heat the tub and the water's temperature would not rise any further.

2.22   The Hold-Up

When the man parked his car outside the bank he held up twenty-five people who were stuck in traffic behind him. The policeman told him not to park like that again.

2.23 The Worst Sailor

The captain would prefer to have ten men like Jim because currently he has fifty men like Jim. He considers almost the entire crew as useless, but is stuck with them for the duration of the voyage!

2.24 The Valuable Book

The man actually owned two copies of the valuable book. By destroying one copy he increased the value of the other.

3 Difficult Puzzles

3.1 Cuddly Bears

The hospital dressed all their teddy bears with bandages. Then they explained to the little children that the poor teddies had to stay at the hospital for their own health and recovery. The children reluctantly but sympathetically agreed.

3.2 The High-Society Dinner

The man who refused to be searched was an aristocrat who had fallen on very hard times but was trying to keep up appearances. He was so poor, however, that he could scarcely afford to eat. So, while at the dinner, he secretly lined his pockets with food from the table to keep him going for the next few days. Obviously if he was searched his secret would be revealed and he would be humiliated.

3.3 Eight Years Old

She was born on February 29, 1896. The year 1900 was not a leap year (only centuries divisible by 400 are leap years), so the next February 29 fell in 1904 when she was eight. She was twelve on her second birthday.

3.4   Cover That Hole

A square or rectangular manhole cover can fall down the hole, while a round manhole cover cannot. The square cover will fit down the diagonal of the hole (unless the rim it sits on is very large) but no matter how you turn a circle it never measures less than its diameter. So for safety and practicality all manhole covers should be round.

3.5   The Protagoras Paradox

This is a paradox with no clear-cut answer. Both parties have a good case. It would be interesting to see it argued out in court. Whoever lost could claim to have won—the student in losing would still not have won a case, Protagoras in losing would ensure a first victory for his pupil.

Some believe that the most likely outcome of such a situation, if it had come to trial, would have been victory for the student. He was after all under no obligation to practise law and up until that point he had not breached the contract. Once Protagoras had lost the first case, however, he could sue a second time on the grounds that the student had now won a case and was in breach of contract. Protagoras would therefore win the second case and recover his fees. Overall, Protagoras would have won.

The student would be smart to choose not to represent himself but to select a good lawyer who could win the first case for him. In that case, since the pupil would still not have won a case, he would have won the contest.

3.6   Hand in Glove

The manufacturer sent 5,000 right-hand gloves to Miami and 5,000 left-hand gloves to New York. He refused to pay the duty on them so both sets of gloves were impounded. Since nobody claimed them, both lots were subsequently sold off at auction. They went for a very low price (who wants 5,000 left-hand gloves?). Naturally, it was the clever Frenchman who won with a very low bid at each auction.

3.7   The School Superintendent

The teacher instructed her pupils always to raise their hands when a question was asked whether they knew the answer or not. If they did not know the answer they should raise their left hand. If they were sure they knew the answer they should raise their right hand. The teacher chose a different child each time, but always one who had raised his or her right hand.

3.8   No Trumps

It is equally likely that one couple will have all the trumps as that they will have no trumps between them. For if they have all the trumps it must mean that the other pair has none and vice versa.

3.9   How to Beat Nick Faldo

The challenger was a blind golfer and he arranged to play the champion at midnight on a dark night. The blind man was at no disadvantage in the dark but the champion could not see his ball to hit it. (Blind golfers do play matches and tournaments; they rely on others to indicate where their ball and the hole are.)

3.10   How to Beat Carl Lewis

He challenged the Olympic champion to run up a ladder. Since he was the fastest window cleaner in Ireland he won easily!

3.11   The Missing Furniture

The man was a circus lion tamer who had unfortunately forgotten his chair when he had to face a bad-tempered lion!

3.12   The Dead Man

The cord around the man's neck was a piece of rawhide

which he had soaked in water before entering the room. Once he had tied it tightly around his neck it naturally grew tighter and tighter as it dried.

3.13   The Busy Hospital

The wearing of seat belts was successful in reducing the number of deaths from road accidents. People who without seat belts would have been killed (and taken to the morgue) now survived but with injuries. Consequently more people were treated for injuries than before.

3.14   The Fallen Sign

The man knew the name of the town he had left that morning. So he replaced the sign so that it correctly named the direction he had come from. It would then be correct for all the other directions.

3.15   False Fingerprints

The man put his wife's big-toe print on the knife and left it beside the body. He could have used his own toe-print but that could have been later traced to him. Once his wife was buried, the "fingerprints" could never be traced.

3.16   Found, Lost, Found

The man fell overboard from a small boat at the seashore. He could not swim well and got into difficulties so he threw away the expensive and heavy binoculars around his neck. He was rescued. He then offered a swimmer a reward to dive down and recover his binoculars. This effort was unsuccessful. Later, however, when the tide went out he was able to pick them up off the sand.

3.17   The Crippled Child

This is a true story from India. The child was born into a family of beggars in Calcutta. The parents knew that a crippled child would earn more as a beggar than a healthy child would.

3.18   Insurance

This is a true story from Japan. The man was a keen golfer and his lifelong ambition was to score a hole in one. But this would prove very expensive as the custom at his golf club was that anyone who scored a hole in one had to buy all the other members a drink.

3.19   Eggs

A spherical or oval egg would roll in a straight line. However, an asymmetrical egg, which is narrower at one end than the other, will tend to roll in a circle. (Try it with a normal hen's egg.) If the eggs are on a cliff edge or other precarious place, the tendency to roll *around* rather than straight is a distinct advantage.

3.20   The Guard Dog

The boy brought along with him a female dog in heat. He released this dog into the orchard and the guard dog was thereby distracted.

3.21   The Last Message

The cassette had started at the beginning of the man's utterance. Who could have rewound it?

3.22   The Japanese Speaker

The businessman had been taught by a woman and he spoke Japanese like a woman. The speech intonation of men and women is very different in Japan, the masculine approach being more direct and aggressive. To hear a man speaking in a woman's style was unusual and amusing for the Japanese men.

4   Fiendish Puzzles

4.1   The Cellar Door

When the girl opened the cellar door she saw the living room and, through its windows, the garden. She had never seen these before because her parents had kept her all her life in the cellar. (This is a true lateral-thinking puzzler as nearly everyone makes the assumption that anyone opening the cellar door does so from outside the cellar.)

4.2   The Deadly Shot

The man died through suffocation. He was covered by an avalanche of snow which had been started by the sound of his gunshot as he stood at the foot of a snow-covered mountain.

4.3   Flat Out

Who said that the car was on the road? The car was being transported on the train.

4.4   An Odd Story

The first man put one lump of sugar in his coffee. That is an odd number. The second man put one lump in his coffee. That is also an odd number. The third man put 10 lumps in his coffee. That is a very odd number of lumps to put into a cup of coffee!

4.5   Free Maps

The aerial photography enabled a much clearer definition of land boundaries, and sizes. A tax on land at that time was based on its estimated area; and these had been largely underestimates. The new maps revealed correct land sizes and the government received more income from the land tax.

4.6   What a Shock I

The man was a prisoner who had been condemned to a very long jail sentence. He paid the prison undertaker to help him escape. The plan was that when the next prisoner died, the man would get into the coffin with the corpse. Later, after the coffin was buried outside the prison walls, the undertaker would dig it up to release the man.

When he heard that a man had died, the prisoner put his plan into action. In the dead of night he climbed into the coffin with the corpse. He fell asleep. He awoke after the burial and lit a match. He then saw that the face of the corpse was that of the undertaker!

4.7   What a Shock II

The man discovered a box containing four glass eyes mounted to a board with a dedication to their previous owners. They had belonged to the four previous husbands of his wife. The men had all died after about a year of marriage. This was the first that he had heard of them. He was recently married and had a glass eye!

4.8   The Deadly Party

The poison in the punch came from the ice cubes in it. When the man drank from the punch the ice had just been added and was still solid. Gradually, during the course of the evening, the ice melted contaminating the punch with the poison.

4.9   Speechless

The two men were both divers. They met one afternoon while scuba diving on the sea bed.

4.10   How to Hug

What the boy had picked up at the library was a volume of an encyclopedia. It was the section covering words beginning with H from How to Hug and that was what was printed on its cover.

4.11 The Healthy Dairymaids

Dairymaids caught the disease cowpox (a relatively harmless disease) from cows. This, however, gave them immunity from the related but much more dangerous disease smallpox. Jenner researched and developed the technique for inoculation with cowpox vaccine which eventually became widespread and overcame the bane of smallpox.

4.12 Toothache

When the man had been very poor he had entered into a contract with a Swedish medical institute. For a certain sum of money he promised them his body after his death for medical research. He later inherited money and asked to buy back this obligation. The institute refused, so he sued them in court. Not only did he lose his case, but the judge ordered him to pay the institute compensation for having had his teeth removed without the permission of their future owners!

4.13 The Lake Problem

You pour into the lake a known quantity of a concentrated chemical or vegetable dye. After allowing some time for the harmless chemical to disperse, you take samples of the water in several places. The more diluted the solution the greater the volume of water in the lake. Precise analysis of the concentration of chemicals in the samples would give a good estimate of the water volume of the lake.

4.14 The Realization

The man had just visited his wife in a hospital. She was on a life-support machine following a car accident. As he was walking down the stairs all the lights went out. There had been a power cut and the emergency back-up systems had failed. He knew immediately that his wife had died.

4.15 The Deadly Dish

The dish that the two men ordered was albatross, to remind themselves of when they had been stranded on a desert island many years earlier. When one of the men tasted it, he realized that he had never tasted albatross before. This meant that the meat he had been given to eat on the island was not albatross, as he had been told, but the flesh of his son who had died when they first reached the island.

4.16   Men in Uniform

The angry man was a convicted prisoner. He was being transported in the van and was handcuffed to a prison officer. When a suitable opportunity arose, the prisoner had produced a gun and demanded that the officer release him. The officer had put the key to the handcuffs in his mouth before struggling with the prisoner. The gun went off killing the officer but not before he had swallowed the key. The prisoner was therefore handcuffed to the body of the man he had just killed.

4.17   Healthy People I

The people were examined using a new technique called X-rays. Up until this time medical understanding of the human body was based largely on the dissection of corpses. This was always done on bodies lying horizontally. X-ray examinations were performed on people who were standing up. The difference caused many internal organs to have a different shape or position. Doctors misread this different appearance under X-ray to diagnose and treat problems which did not exist. They did not think laterally!

4.18   Healthy People II

The hospital was a maternity hospital and all those admitted were pregnant women.

4.19 The Grand Prix

Although the driver could not himself see around the curve, he could see the crowd in the stands ahead looking intently round the bend. He reasoned that they were not looking at him, a world-famous racing driver, because something more interesting, possibly a crash, had occurred around the curve.

4.20 The Stranger in the Car

The woman had died in childbirth. The stranger was the man's newborn son.

4.21 Eggshell Finish

The man was a professional clown. Each clown tries to have a unique face and copyrights his clown face by painting it on an eggshell which is then deposited with the international clown's club.

About the Authors

Paul Sloane was born in Scotland and grew up near Blackpool in the north of England. He studied Engineering at Trinity Hall, Cambridge, and graduated with a first-class honors degree. While at Cambridge he met his wife, who is a teacher. They live in Camberley, England, with their three daughters.

Most of Paul Sloane's career has been in the computer industry and he is currently the European vice-president for a software company. He has always been an avid collector and creator of puzzles. His first book, *Lateral Thinking Puzzlers,* was published by Sterling in 1991. Paul Sloane has given speeches and radio talks on the topic of change management and lateral thinking.

Des MacHale was born in County Mayo, Ireland, and is Associate Professor of Mathematics at University College in Cork. He was educated at University College, Galway, and the University of Keele in England. He and his wife, Anne, have five children.

The author of over thirty books, mostly of humor but also one on giving up smoking, Des MacHale has many interests including puzzles, geology, writing, broadcasting, films, photography, numismatics, and, of course, mathematics. He is currently working on three more books.

Sharing a strong interest in jokes and puzzles, and following a chance meeting in 1991, **Paul Sloane** and **Des MacHale** decided to cooperate on a book of problems. This work is the result.

PUZZLE INDEX

Page key: **puzzle**, *clue*, solution